ARCHIPELAGO

Archipelago

Arthur Sze

COPPER CANYON PRESS

Publication of this book is supported by a grant from the National
Endowment for the Arts and a grant from the Lannan Foundation.
Additional support to Copper Canyon Press has been provided by the
Andrew W. Mellon Foundation, the Lila Wallace–Reader's Digest Fund,
and the Washington State Arts Commission. Copper Canyon Press is
in residence with Centrum at Fort Worden State Park.

Library of Congress Cataloging-in-Publication Data
Sze, Arthur, 1950–
Archipelago / Arthur Sze
p. cm.
ISBN 1-55659-100-4
1. Gardens, Japanese – Zen influences – Poetry. 2. Chinese Americans –
Poetry. 3. Zen poetry, American. I. Title.
PS3569.Z38A89 1995
811'.54 – DC20   95-17228

0 9 8 7 6 5 4 3 2 1

COPPER CANYON PRESS
P.O. BOX 271, PORT TOWNSEND, WASHINGTON 98368

100297-1056 K8

Grateful acknowledgment is made to the editors of the following publications in which these poems, sometimes in earlier versions, first appeared:

The American Poetry Review: "The Redshifting Web"
Asian America: "The Shapes of Leaves"
B City: "A Great Square Has No Corners"
Caliban: "The Los Alamos Museum"
Chelsea: "Axolotl," "The Great White Shark," "In Your Honor"
Contact II: "From the Rooftop"
First Intensity: "X Ray"
Hanging Loose: "Spring Snow"
The Kenyon Review: "Oolong"
Manoa: "The Flower Path," "Mushroom Hunting in the Jemez Mountains,"
      "Original Memory," "The Silk Road," "Slanting Light"
The Paris Review: "Archipelago," "Streamers"
Quarry West: "Ice Floe," "Whiteout"
River Styx: "Rattlesnake Glyph"
The Taos Review: "Red Octopus"
American Poets Say Goodbye to the Twentieth Century (*Exquisite Corpse*,
      Four Walls Eight Windows Press): "Streamers"
Kyoto Journal: "Oolong," sections 1, 2, 3, 7, and "Spring Snow"
New Mexico Poetry Renaissance (Red Crane Books): "The Flower Path,"
      "From the Rooftop," "Original Memory," "Whiteout"
Premonitions: The Kaya Anthology of New Asian North American Poetry
      (Kaya Production): "Archipelago," "The Los Alamos Museum"
Today (Oxford University Press): "Archipelago," sections 1, 3, 4, 5 translated
      into Chinese by Janet Tan.

"The Flower Path" also appeared in *Archive Newsletter*, and "The Silk Road" appeared as a broadside from Light and Dust Books.

I wish to thank the George A. and Eliza Gardner Howard Foundation, the National Endowment for the Arts, and the Witter Bynner Foundation for Poetry, for their fellowships, as well as the New Mexico Arts Division for an interdisciplinary grant, all of which were a great help in writing this book.

v

For Mona

CONTENTS

ARCHIPELAGO

STREAMERS

1   As an archaeologist unearths a mask with opercular teeth
and abalone eyes, someone throws a broken fan and extension
      cords
into a dumpster. A point of coincidence exists in the mind

resembling the tension between a denotation and its stretch
of definition: aurora: a luminous phenomenon consisting
of streamers or arches of light appearing in the upper
      atmosphere

of a planet's polar regions, caused by the emission of light
from atoms excited by electrons accelerated along the planet's
magnetic field lines. The mind's magnetic field lines.

When the red shimmering in the huge dome of sky stops,
a violet flare is already arcing up and across, while a man
foraging a dumpster in Cleveland finds some celery and
      charred fat.

Hunger, angst: the blue shimmer of emotion, water speeding
through a canyon; to see only to know: to wake finding
a lug nut, ticket stub, string, personal card, ink smear, $2.76.

2   A Kwakiutl wooden dish with a double-headed wolf
     is missing from a museum collection. And as

        the director checks to see if it was deaccessioned,
        a man sitting on a stool under bright lights

        shouts: a pachinko ball dropped vertiginously
        but struck a chiming ring and ricocheted to the left.

        We had no sense that a peony was opening,
        that a thousand white buds of a Kyoto camellia

        had opened at dusk and had closed at dawn.
        When the man steps out of the pachinko parlor,

        he will find himself vertiginously dropping
        in starless space. When he discovers

        that his daughter was cooking over smoking oil
        and shrieked in a fatal asthma attack,

        he will walk the bright streets in an implosion of grief,
        his mind will become an imploding star,

        he will know he is searching among bright gold threads
        for a black pattern in the weave.

3   Set a string loop into a figure of two diamonds,
     four diamonds, one diamond:
     as a woman tightens her hand into a fist
     and rubs it in a circular motion over her heart,
     a bewildered man considering the semantics of *set*
     decides no through-line exists:

     to sink the head of a nail below the surface,
     to fix as a distinguishing imprint, sign, or appearance,
     to incite, put on a fine edge by grinding,
     to adjust, adorn, put in motion, make unyielding,
     to bend slightly the tooth points of a saw
     alternately in opposite directions.

     As the woman using her index finger makes
     spiral after spiral from her aorta up over her head,
     see the possibilities for transcendence:
     you have to die and die in your mind
     before you can begin to see the empty spaces
     the configuration of string defines.

4   A restorer examines the pieces of a tin chandelier,
and notices the breaks in the arms are along
old solder lines, and that cheap epoxy was used.

He will have to scrape off the epoxy, scrub some flux,
heat up the chandelier and use a proper solder.
A pair of rough-legged hawks are circling over a pasture;

one hawk cuts off the rabbit's path of retreat
while the other swoops with sharp angle and curve of wings.
Cirrus, cirrostratus, cirrocumulus, altostratus,

altocumulus, stratocumulus, nimbostratus,
cumulus, cumulonimbus, stratus: is there no end?
Memories stored in the body begin to glow.

A woman seals basil in brown bags and hangs them
from the ceiling. A dead sturgeon washes to shore.
The sun is at the horizon, but another sun

is rippling in water. It's not that the angle
of reflection equals the angle of incidence,
but there's exultation, pleasure, distress, death, love.

5   The world resembles a cuttlefish changing colors
    and shimmering. An apprentice archer has

    stretched the bowstring properly, but does not know
    he will miss the target because he is not aiming in the hips.

    He will learn to hit the target without aiming
    when he has died in his mind. I am not scared of death,

    though I am appalled at how obsession with security
    yields a pin-pushing, pencil-shaving existence.

    You can descend to the swimming level of sharks,
    be a giant kelp growing from the ocean bottom up

    to the surface light, but the critical moment
    is to die feeling the infinite stillness of the passions,

    to revel in the touch of hips, hair, lips, hands,
    feel the collapse of space in December light.

    When I know I am no longer trying to know the spectral lines
    of the earth, I can point to a cuttlefish and say,

    "Here it is sepia," already it is deep-brown,
    and exult, "Here it is deep-brown," already it is white.

6   Red koi swim toward us, and black
     carp are rising out of the depths of the pond,
     but our sustenance is a laugh, a grief,

     a walk at night in the snow,
     seeing the pure gold of a flickering candle –
     a moment at dusk when we see

     that deer have been staring at us,
     we did not see them edge out of the brush,
     a moment when someone turns on a light

     and turns a window into a mirror,
     a moment when a child asks,
     "When will it be tomorrow?"

     To say "A bell cannot be red and violet
     at the same place and time because
     of the logical structure of color" is true

     but is a dot that must enlarge into
     a zero: a void, *enso*, red shimmer,
     breath, endless beginning, pure body, pure mind.

O

THE SILK ROAD

1   The blood in your arteries is contaminated with sugar.
You may hate the adrenal reduction of the mind to

the mind of a dog, but *sic, run* may be forms of sugar.
You may whet for the smell of rain on a clear summer night.

You may whet for the sugar in red maple leaves.
You may whet for the blue needle of a compass to point

north, and when it points north insist you wanted it
to point north-northwest. No, yes. In a dream

you catch a white turtle in a net and a voice says,
"Kill it, divine with it, and you shall have good luck,"

but discard dream structure for a deeper asymmetry.
You thirst in your mind for an insulin, death:

death in the yellow saguaro flower opening at midnight,
death in a canyon wren's song at sunrise,

death in red carp swimming in a clear pool of water,
death in an April moonrise. Now the figure-of-eight knot,

overhand knot, thief knot, loop knot, bowline knot,
slide knot, slipknot, sheepshank is pulled tighter and tighter.

2   You may stare out of a south window for hours
    and feel the April sunlight dissolve the shifting leaves,

    and you may dream sunlight opening a red camellia.
    You may eat monkey brains and bear paws,

    but, out of disordered passions and a disordered mind,
    can you construct yellow doors that open in silence into
        summer?

    You may repeat mistake after mistake so that you
    will the mistakes into an accelerating spiral of despair.

    A turtle pushes onto the sand of Bikini Island,
    and, disoriented by radiation, pushes further and further

    inland to die; but do not confuse the bones
    of a cow bleached in the sun with disordered desire.

    You may dream sunlight shining into a cool mountain forest
    and wake up inhaling the smell of Douglas fir.

    You may dream sea turtles swimming in black water
    but wake sunstruck walking in shifting dunes of white sand.

    Who can say *here, now* is metempsychosic delusion?
    Can you set out for Turfan today and arrive yesterday at dusk?

3   A man in a hospital is waiting for a heart transplant.
He may fish at night under the stars with a cool salt wind;

he may soar out over the black shining waters of a bay.
He may want to die with sunlight shining on his face;

he may want to die in a tsunami, but his yes and his no
are a void. He may die as a gray squirrel cracks open an acorn;

he may die as a green terrapin slips into a stream.
As a diabetic shivers and sweats, shivers and sweats,

he feels the moonlight shining on the high tide waters of the bay.
He feels the drone of traffic slip into silence, and then

the trivial, the inconsequential stings him, stings him.
As a child, he said to his father, "That man is weird;

why does he wear a pillow under his pants?" And his father
    laughed,
"He's fat, so fat." Then, "The Chinese word for onion

is *cong*, so a green onion is *xiao cong*, small onion, yes?"
"Yes." "Then a large white onion must be *da cong*, large

onion, yes?" "No, a large white onion is called *yang cong*."
"*Yang cong*?" "Yes." "Which *yang*?" "The *yang* that means *ocean*."
    "Shit."

4   The, a, this, the, tangerine, splash, hardly:
     these threads of sound may be spun in s-spin into fiber:

     lighted buoy, whistling buoy, spar buoy, bell buoy, buoy.
     Hear the sounds of apricots dropping from branches to the earth;

     feel the red vibration of wings before you see a hummingbird.
     A man may travel from Mindanao to Macao to avoid

     staring into himself; he may search at night in a helicopter
     for the shimmer of a fire opal dropped into water;

     he may inhale starlight as if it were a pungent yellow
     flower opening slowly in the still August night.

     To be still: watch a dog listen to sounds you cannot hear,
     feel the pull of moonrise on the feathers of an owl.

     There are apricots beginning to drop from branches to the earth;
     there are apricots not yet beginning to drop from branches;

     there are apricots not yet not yet beginning to drop.

5   This sand was black and silver shining in the megalight.
Now the radiation is in my hands and in your face.

You may dream red petals on a mountain path in rain;
I may watch the shimmer of light in the yellowing leaves.

Yes and no, spring and autumn have no power without the mind
that wills them into magnetic north, magnetic south.

A merchant from Xi'an brought ceremonial caps to Kuqa,
but the Kuqa people shaved their heads and tattooed their bodies.

To seal a dime in a red envelope and send it to
an insurance salesman is to send anthurium to a cannibal.

The taste of unripe persimmons, and pale moonlight shining
on the black hills appear to have no use: who

would have dreamed they would become, *shibui*, an aesthetic?
To argue that you must know the characteristic

that makes all birds birds before you can identify
a bird – and here you must discard antinomies –

postpones *auk* to that indeterminate time in the fallout
of the future when you shall have knowledge of the form *Death*.

6   Various proofs for the existence of God
     try to predicate existence, but being

          is unlike *yellow, sour, pungent.* That a branch
          of the linden has yellow and dropping

          leaves hardly enables us to infer that
          water flowing through the underground *karez*

          into Turfan is about to stop. If
          the passions are the music of empty holes,

          hear the blue and gold sounds of angst.
          As I stared out the south window, I

          saw the leaves of the linden green with no hint
          of yellow. No, as I stared out the south

          window, I wanted to see the yellowing leaves,
          but instead saw, reflected in the glass

          back through the space of the room
          and out another window, salted skates

          hanging on a wire to dry. So what I saw
          reflected deflected my intention as now I say *now.*

O

OOLONG

1   Tea leaves wilted in sunlight are shaken
      and bruised so that the edges redden
      and veins turn transparent. A man at a counter
      eats boiled silkworms and coughs;
      a woman stops speaking and stares
      at the constellation Perseus. Once,
      a merchant smashed a black raku bowl
      when it failed to please a tea master,
      but, glued back together, the black shards
      had the texture of mulberry leaves.
      You pass someone bowing talking on the telephone,
      and the shock is an incandescent quark
      leaving a spiraling track in the mind:
      you sense how, in a field guide, it is impossible
      to know the growth arc of a mushroom,
      but stumble upon shelves of oysters
      growing out of dead aspens and
      see how nothing in this world is yet yours.

2   True or false:

termites release methane and add to the greenhouse effect;

the skin of a blowfish is lethal;

crosses along roads in Mexico mark vehicular deaths;

the earth is flat;

oysters at full moon contain hepatitis;

no one has ever seen a neutrino;

butterflies dream;

the fins of a blowfish are always edible;

oolong means *black dragon*, but *oo* means *crow* and *long* means
    dragon;

he loved the curves of her body;

the sun revolves around the earth;

caffeine stimulates the central nervous system;

light is a wave;

the mind is composed of brightest bright and darkest dark;

context is crucial;

pfennigs, xu, qindarka, centimes, stotinki, qursh are coins;

the raw liver of a tiger blowfish
caught at winter solstice is a delicacy;

I have a knife inscribed with the names of forty-eight fish.

3   You sift curtains of red light
     shimmering in the November sky,
     sift the mind of a roofer mopping hot tar.
     Walking down a hallway, you stop

     and sift the brains in a glass bowl,
     sift the tag dangling from the wrist of a corpse,
     sift the folded wings of a sparrow.
     The prevailing notions of the season

     are green-stained lactarius prevailing
     in the mountains for three days and an hour.
     You have to reject ideas of disjunction
     and collage, reject advice, praise.

     Then you might look at a Song dynasty map
     of Hangzhou and see the configuration
     of ion channels in the brain. You might look
     at an aboriginal sandpainting and see

     a cosmology of grief. You might look
     at the swaying motion of a branch
     and feel what it is to be a
     burned and shriveled leaf clinging to death.

4   I stare into a black bowl and smell
whisked green tea, see a flap of tails
and orange koi surging in a stream.
Sunlight is dropping down through tallest pines;
I stop on a bridge, and water
passes underneath and through me.
As a potter has a premonition of death
when he avoids using a red glaze on a square dish,
we come to know the form and pressure of an emotion
when it's gone: a soliloquy of despair
ends as a rope burn in the hands,
and pleasure flares into a gold chrysanthemum.
Is the spinning spinless when nothing is yours?
The mind slows to a green-flecked swirl;
I touch contours of the black shards.
Before sunrise, a man is cutting all
the morning glories blooming in the garden
and places one in a jar in a tearoom.

5   They smuggled his corpse into the city in a pile of rotting
        abalone;

"Very famous": they all nodded;

he knew the daphne was a forbidden flower;

"Twerp," a restaurant inspector muttered
and placed a C in the window;

they slurped noodles and read comic books;

he spits off the subway platform;

the slightest noise so disturbed him he had a soundproof room
    built:
white walls, white floor;

she kept feeling a snail on her neck;

for tea ceremony,
he cut three gentians and threw them into an Acoma pot;

she buried the placenta in the cornfield;

a hunter discovers a honey mushroom larger than a blue whale;

what opens and closes, closes and opens?

she took his breath away;

he dips his brush
and writes the character "flower" incorporating the character
    "mind";

a flayed elephant skin;

she stir-fries tea leaves in a wok.

6   Red poppies are blooming along a wall;
I look at green and underlying blue paint
peeling off a bench: you rummage in a shed
and find a spindle, notice the oil of
hands has accumulated on the shaft.
In the rippling shadows, the shimmer of water.
I see yellow iris in a vase on the kitchen table
and smell lightning; commuters at the World
Trade Center may descend escalators to subways:
it is always 5:05; Su-wei brought him
five thousand yellow pills and said if
he swallowed twelve each day it would
restore his hair, but is this a form of
sipping sake steeped in a jar full of vipers?
Footprints under water in a rice paddy
and on the water's surface, clouds;
Altair and Vega spin in longing:
the sun dips below the horizon in a watery gold.

7   The mycelium of a honey mushroom
      glows in the dark. What does a yellow
      Man On Horseback know of winter and spring?
      A farmer pushes his fist into clay

      and forms a bowl. The world will continue
      as long as two aborigines
      clack boomerangs and chant?
      A woman has the watery shine

      of a sapphire and becomes yellow lightning.
      She has a dream that resembles a geode:
      if we could open it we might
      recover the hue of the first world.

      The light through a pressed octopus cup
      has a rippling texture resembling
      a cool undulating shadow over skin.
      In the dark, the precession

      and nutation of an emotion is a star:
      Sirius, Arcturus, Capella, Procyon, Aldebaran:
      shadows of mosquitoes are moving
      along a rice paper screen.

O

IN YOUR HONOR

In your honor, a man presents a sea bass
tied to a black-lacquered dish by green-spun seaweed.

"Ah" is heard throughout the room:
you are unsure what is about to happen.

You might look through a telescope at the full
bright moon against deep black space,

see from the Bay of Dew to the Sea of Nectar,
but, no, this beauty of naming is a subterfuge.

What are the thoughts of hunters driving
home on a Sunday afternoon empty-handed?

Their conception of honor may coincide
with your conception of cruelty? The slant

of light as sun declines is a knife
separating will and act into infinitely thin

and lucid slices. You look at the sea bass's eye,
clear and luminous. The gills appear to move

ever so slightly. The sea bass smells
of dream, but this is no dream. "Ah,

such delicacy" is heard throughout the room,
and the sea bass suddenly flaps. It

bleeds and flaps, bleeds and flaps as
the host slices slice after slice of glistening sashimi.

Down to this north end of the verandah, across the view
of 1,001 gold-leafed statues of Kuan-yin looking west,
Wasa Daihachiro, in twenty-four hours in 1686, shot
13,054 arrows of which 8,133 were bull's eyes. Today
no one can pull the two hundred pound laminated bamboo bow
to send a single arrow with a low trajectory the length
of the thirty-three bays. As you walk on the verandah,
you see a tree full of white bags tied over peaches,
hear the sound of bells at a fish auction,
note the stares of men sitting on tiers under lights;
you are careful not to raise your hand as you examine
a two hundred pound tuna smoking just unpacked from dry ice;
at lunch you put a shrimp in your mouth and feel it twitch;
you enter a house and are dazed as your eyes adjust to
a hundred blind Darumas in the room;
you must learn to see a pond in the shape of the character "mind,"
walk through a garden and see it from your ankles;
a family living behind a flower arrangement shop
presents the store as a face to the street;
the eldest daughter winces when the eighty-year-old parents
get out wedding pictures of the second daughter;
at night the belching sounds of frogs;
in the morning you look in rice paddies and find only tadpoles;
you are walking down into a gorge along the river,
turn to find stone piled on stone offerings along the path
and on rocks in midstream; in the depths of the cave,
a gold mirror with candles burning;
deer running at dusk in a dry moat;
iris blooming and about to bloom;
you are walking across Moon-Crossing Bridge in slashing rain,

meet a Rinzai monk with a fax machine
who likes to crank up a Victrola with a gold horn;
you see the red ocher upper walls of a teahouse,
and below the slatted bamboo fences called "dog repellers";
you stop at the south end of the verandah and look north;
an actor walks off the flower path ramp cross-eyed amid shouts.

THE GREAT WHITE SHARK

For days he has dumped a trail of tuna blood
into the ocean so that a great white shark

might be lured, so that we might touch its fin.
The power of the primitive is parallactic:

in a museum exhibit, a *chacmool* appears as elegant
and sophisticated sculpture, as art, but

witness the priest rip the still-beating heart
out of the blue victim's body and place it

pulsing on a *chacmool* and we are ready to vomit.
We think the use of a beryllium gyroscope

marks technological superiority, but the urge
of ideologies then and now makes revenge inexorable.

The urge to skydive, rappel, white-water kayak
is the urge to release, the urge to die.

Diamond and graphite may be allotropic forms
of carbon, but what are the allotropic forms

of ritual and desire? The moon shining on black water,
yellow forsythia blossoming in the April night,

red maple leaves dropping in silence in October:
the seasons are not yet human forms of desire.

SLANTING LIGHT

Slanting light casts onto a stucco wall
the shadows of upwardly zigzagging plum branches.

I can see the thinning of branches to the very twig.
I have to sift what you say, what she thinks,

what he believes is genetic strength, what
they agree is inevitable. I have to sift this

quirky and lashing stillness of form to see myself,
even as I see laid out on a table for Death

an assortment of pomegranates and gourds.
And what if Death eats a few pomegranate seeds?

Does it insure a few years of pungent spring?
I see one gourd, yellow from midsection to top

and zucchini-green lower down, but
already the big orange gourd is gnawed black.

I have no idea why the one survives the killing nights.
I have to sift what you said, what I felt,

what you hoped, what I knew. I have to sift
death as the stark light sifts the branches of the plum.

She folds the four corners into the center,
hears the sound of a porcupine in a cornfield,
smells heart-shaped leaves in the dark.
She stops, noticing she has folded the red side out.
She is supposed to fold so that the red is seen
through white as what lies below surface.

So she restarts and folds the creases in air.
She recalls her mother arguing and flashing her party card;
she recalls soldiers at the Great Hall of the People
receive medals; she recalls her father film
a chimpanzee smoking a cigarette at the Beijing zoo;
she senses how the soldiers were betrayed.

She makes a petal fold, a valley fold,
an open-sink fold, a series of mountain folds,
pondering how truths were snared by malice.
She makes an inside reverse fold, crimps the legs,
and, with a quick spurt of air,
inflates the body of the octopus.

WHITEOUT

You expect to see swirling chunks of ice
flowing south toward open water of the ocean,
but, no, a moment of whiteout as
the swirling ice flows north at sunset.
In a restaurant with an empty screen,
a woman gets up and sings a Chinese song
with "empty orchestra" accompaniment.
Prerecorded music fills the room,
and projection from a laser disc throws
a waterfall and red hibiscus onto the screen.
You are not interested in singing and
following the words as they change color
from yellow to purple across the cueing machine.
Instead, you walk out on blue-green glacier
ice and feel it thin to water in spring.
You notice two moose along the thawing shoreline
browsing for buds, and see the posted sign
"No shooting from here." But "here" is "there."

Nails dropped off a roof onto flagstone;
slow motion shatter of a windowpane;
the hushed sound when a circular saw cutting through plywood
stops, and splinters of wood are drifting in air;
lipstick graffiti on a living room wall;
cold stinging your eardrums;
braking suddenly along a curve, and the car spinning,
holding your breath as the side-view mirror is snapped by a
    sign pole;
the snap as a purple chalk line marks an angular cut on black
    Cellutex;
dirt under your nails,
as you dig up green onions with your bare hands;
fiber plaster setting on a wall;
plugging in an iron and noticing the lights dim in the other room;
sound of a pencil drawn along the edge of a trisquare;
discovering your blurred vision is caused by having two contacts
    in each eye;
thud as the car slams into a snowbank and hits a fence;
smell of a burnt yam;
the bones of your wrist being crushed;
under a geranium leaf, a mass of spiders
moving slowly on tiny threads up and down and across to
    different stems.

In this museum is a replica of "Little Boy" and "Fat Man." In "Little Boy," a radar echo set off an explosive which drove a uranium-235 wedge into a larger uranium target, while in "Fat Man" the ordinary explosive crushed a hollow sphere of plutonium into a beryllium core. To the right of these replicas, a computer gives you the opportunity to design a reentry missile out of aluminum or steel. The reentry point of the aluminum missile needs to be thicker than the steel one, but, because it has a lighter atomic weight, when you push the button choosing the aluminum design, the computer rewards you with blinking lights and sounds. Further on in the main room, a model with lights shows the almost instantaneous release of neutrons and gamma rays from point zero. At point zero, radiant energy is released at the speed of light, but you can see it here in slow motion.

SPRING SNOW

A spring snow coincides with plum blossoms.
In a month, you will forget, then remember
when nine ravens perched in the elm sway in wind.

I will remember when I brake to a stop,
and a hubcap rolls through the intersection.
An angry man grinds pepper onto his salad;

it is how you nail a tin amulet ear
into the lintel. If, in deep emotion, we are
possessed by the idea of possession,

we can never lose to recover what is ours.
Sounds of an abacus are amplified and condensed
to resemble sounds of hail on a tin roof,

but mind opens to the smell of lightning.
Bodies were vaporized to shadows by intense heat;
in memory people outline bodies on walls.

O

1   The dragons on the back of a circular bronze mirror
     swirl without end. I sit and am an absorbing form:
     I absorb the outline of a snowy owl on a branch,
     the rigor mortis in a hand. I absorb the crunching sounds
     when you walk across a glacial lake with aquamarine
     ice heaved up here and there twenty feet high.
     I absorb the moment a jeweler pours molten gold
     into a cuttlefish mold and it begins to smoke.
     I absorb the weight of a pause when it tilts
     the conversation in a room. I absorb the moments
     he sleeps holding her right breast in his left hand
     and know it resembles glassy waves in a harbor
     in descending spring light. Is the mind a mirror?
     I see pig carcasses piled up from the floor
     on a boat docked at Wanxian and the cook
     who smokes inadvertently drops ashes into soup.
     I absorb the stench of burning cuttlefish bone,
     and as moments coalesce see to travel far is to return.

2   A cochineal picker goes blind;

Mao, swimming across the Yangtze River,
was buoyed by underwater frogmen;

in the nursing home,
she yelled, "Everyone here has Alzheimer's!"

it blistered his mouth;

they thought the tape of *erhu* solos was a series of spy messages;

finding a bag of piki pushpinned to the door;

shapes of saguaros by starlight;

a yogi tries on cowboy boots at a flea market;

a peregrine falcon
shears off a wing;

her niece went through the house and took what she wanted;

"The sooner the better";

like a blindman grinding the bones of a snow leopard;

she knew you had come to cut her hair;

suffering: this and that:

iron 26, gold 79;

they dared him to stare at the annular eclipse;

the yellow pupils of a saw-whet owl.

3   The gold shimmer at the beginning of summer
      dissolves in a day. A fly mistakes a
      gold spider, the size of a pinhead, at the center
      of a glistening web. A morning mushroom
      knows nothing of twilight and dawn?
      Instead of developing a navy, Ci Xi
      ordered architects to construct a two story
      marble boat that floats on a lotus-covered lake.
      Mistake a death cap for Caesar's amanita
      and in hours a hepatic hole opens into the sky.
      To avoid yelling at his pregnant wife,
      a neighbor installs a boxing bag in a storeroom;
      he periodically goes in, punches, punches,
      reappears and smiles. A hummingbird moth
      hovers and hovers at a woman wearing a
      cochineal-dyed flowery dress. Liu Hansheng
      collects hypodermic needles, washes them
      under a hand pump, dries them in sunlight,
      seals them in Red Cross plastic bags,
      resells them as sterilized new ones to hospitals.

4   Absorb a corpse-like silence and be a brass
     cone at the end of a string beginning
     to mark the x of stillness. You may puzzle
     as to why a meson beam oscillates, or why
     galaxies appear to be simultaneously redshifting
     in all directions, but do you stop to sense
     death pulling and pulling from the center
     of the earth to the end of the string?
     A mother screams at her son, "You're so stupid,"
     but the motion of this anger is a circle.
     A teen was going to attend a demonstration,
     but his parents, worried about tear gas,
     persuaded him to stay home: he was bludgeoned
     to death that afternoon by a burglar.
     I awake dizzy with a searing headache
     thinking what nightmare did I have
     that I cannot remember only to discover
     the slumlord dusted the floor with roach powder.

5   Moored off Qingdao, before sunrise,
      the pilot of a tanker is selling dismantled bicycles.
      Once, a watchmaker coated numbers on the dial

      with radioactive paint and periodically
      straightened the tip of the brush in his mouth.
      Our son sights the North Star through a straw

      taped to a protractor so that a bolt
      dangling from a string marks the latitude.
      I remember when he said his first word, "Clock";

      his 6:02 is not mine, nor is your 7:03 his.
      We visit Aurelia in the nursing home and find
      she is sleeping curled in a fetal position.

      A chain-smoking acupuncturist burps, curses;
      a teen dips his head in paint thinner.
      We think, had I *this* then that would,

      but subjunctive form is surge and ache.
      Yellow tips of chamisa are flaring open.
      I drop a jar of mustard, and it shatters in a wave.

6   The smell of roasted chili;

descending into the epilimnion;

the shape of a datura leaf;

a bank robber superglued his fingertips;

in the lake,
ocean-seal absorption;

a moray snaps up a scorpion fish;

he had to mistake and mistake;

burned popcorn;

he lifted the fly agaric off of blue paper
and saw a white galaxy;

sitting in a cold sweat;

a child drinking Coke out of a formula bottle
has all her teeth capped in gold;

chrysanthemum-shaped fireworks exploding over the water;

red piki passed down a ladder;

laughter;

as a lobster mold transforms a russula into a delicacy;

replicating an Anasazi
yucca fiber and turkey-feather blanket.

7   He looks at a series of mirrors: Warring States,
        Western Han, Eastern Han, Tang, Song,
        and notices bits of irregular red corrosion

        on the Warring States mirror. On the back,
        three dragons swirl in mist and April air.
        After sixteen years that first kiss

        still has a flaring tail. He looks at the TLV
        pattern on the back of the Han mirror:
        the mind has diamond points east, south, west, north.

        He grimaces and pulls up a pile of potatoes,
        notices snow clouds coming in from the west.
        She places a sunflower head on the northwest

        corner of the fence. He looks at the back
        of the Tang mirror: the lion and grape
        pattern is so wrought he turns, watches her

        pick eggplant, senses the underlying
        twist of pleasure and surprise that
        in mind they flow and respond endlessly.

8   I find a rufous hummingbird on the floor
of a greenhouse, sense a redshifting
along the radial string of a web.
You may draw a cloud pattern in cement
setting in a patio, or wake to
sparkling ferns melting on a windowpane.
The struck, plucked, bowed, blown
sounds of the world come and go.
As first light enters a telescope
and one sees light of a star when the star
has vanished, I see a finch at a feeder,
beans germinating in darkness;
a man with a pole pulls yarn out
of an indigo vat, twists and untwists it;
I hear a shout as a child finds *Boletus
barrowsii* under ponderosa pine;
I see you wearing an onyx and gold pin.
In curved space, is a line a circle?

9 Pausing in the motion of a stroke,
two right hands
grasping a brush;

staring through a skylight
at a lunar eclipse;

a great blue heron,
wings flapping,
landing on the rail of a float house;

near and far:
a continuous warp;

a neighbor wants to tear down this fence;
a workman covets it
for a *trastero*;

raccoons on the rooftop
eating apricots;

the character *xuan* –
dark, dyed –
pinned to a wall above a computer;

lovers making
a room glow;

weaving on a vertical loom:

sound of a comb,
baleen;

    hiding a world in a world:
    1054, a supernova.

O

X RAY

In my mind a lilac begins to leaf

before it begins to leaf.
A new leaf

is a new moon.
As the skin of a chameleon

reflects temperature, light, emotion,
an x ray of my hands

reflects chance, intention, hunger?
You can, in x-ray
diffraction,
study the symmetry of crystals,

but here, now,
the caesura marks a shift in the mind,

the vicissitudes
of starlight,

a luna moth opening its wings.

RATTLESNAKE GLYPH

Curve of the earth in emerald water
deepening into blue where water breaks along

the outer edge of a reef. A snake of equinoctial
light is beginning to descend the nine tiers

of a pyramid. You hear a shout reverberate
down the walls of a ball court, find blood

snakes spurting out of the neck of a decapitated man,
the carved stone ring through which a human head

used as a ball must pass. Here is a wall of
a thousand white sculptured stone skulls

and row after row of heads mounted on spikes.
The darkness drops a mosquito net over a bed:

in blood scroll skull light, I taste the salt
on your skin and in your hair. We are

a rattlesnake glyph aligning memory, dream, desire.
At dawn the slashing sounds of rain turn out

to be wind in the palms. Waves are breaking white
on the reef. Soon turtles will arrive and lay

eggs in the sand. A line of leaf-cutting ants
are passing bits of shiny green leaves across a trail.

"Cut."
An actress feigning death for one hundred seconds gasps.
A man revs
and races a red Mustang up and down the street.
"Cut."

A potter opens a hillside kiln;
he removes a molten bowl,
and, dipping it
in cold water,
it hisses, turns black, cracks.

In despair, a pearl is a sphere.
"Cut."
In Bombay, a line of ear cleaners are standing in a street.
On a mesa top,
the south windows of a house shatter;

underground uranium miners
are releasing explosives.
"Cut."
A rope beginning to unravel in the mind
is, like red antlers,

the axis of a dream.
"Cut."
What is the secret to stopping time?
A one-eyed calligrapher
writes with a mop, "A great square has no corners."

AXOLOTL

I may practice divination with the bones
of an eel, but the world would be
just as cruel were it within my will.

The yellowing leaves of the honey locust
would still be yellowing, and a woman
riding in a hearse would still grieve and grieve.

We don't live in a hypothetical world,
and yet the world would be nothing
without hypothetical dreaming. I hope no

ultimate set of laws to nature exists;
maybe, instead, there's only layering.
Maybe you look in a store window and see

twenty-four televisions with twenty-four images:
now the explosion of a napalm bomb,
now the face of an axolotl.

MUSHROOM HUNTING IN THE JEMEZ MOUNTAINS

Walking in a mountain meadow toward the north slope,
I see redcap amanitas with white warts and know
they signal cèpes. I see a few colonies of puffballs,
red russulas with chalk-white stipes, brown-gilled
Poison Pie. In the shade under spruce are two
red-pored boletes: slice them in half and the flesh
turns blue in seconds. Under fir is a single amanita
with basal cup, flaring annulus, white cap: is it
the Rocky Mountain form of *Amanita pantherina*?
I am aware of danger in naming, in misidentification,
in imposing the distinctions of a taxonomic language
onto the things themselves. I know I have only
a few hours to hunt mushrooms before early afternoon rain.
I know it is a mistake to think I am moving and
that agarics are still: they are more transient
than we acknowledge, more susceptible to full moon,
to a single rain, to night air, to a moment of sunshine.
I know in this meadow my passions are mycorrhizal
with nature. I may shout out ecstasies, aches, griefs,
and hear them vanish in the white-pored silence.

FROM THE ROOFTOP

He wakes up to the noise of ravens in the spruce trees.
For a second, in the mind, the parsley is already
bolting in the heat, but then he realizes
the mind focusing rays into a burning point of light
can also relax its intensity, and then
he feels the slow wave of the day.
Mullein growing by the gas meter
is as significant as the portulaca blooming in pots.
Ants are marching up the vine onto the stucco wall
and into the roof. From the rooftop,
he contemplates the pattern of lightning to the west,
feels a nine-pointed buck edge closer to the road at dusk,
weighs a leaf and wonders what is significant,
maybe the neighbor who plays the saxophone
at odd hours, loudly and badly, but with such expanse.

THE SHAPES OF LEAVES

Ginkgo, cottonwood, pin oak, sweet gum, tulip tree:
our emotions resemble leaves and alive
to their shapes we are nourished.

Have you felt the expanse and contours of grief
along the edges of a big Norway maple?
Have you winced at the orange flare

searing the curves of a curling dogwood?
I have seen from the air logged islands,
each with a network of branching gravel roads,

and felt a moment of pure anger, aspen gold.
I have seen sandhill cranes moving in an open field,
a single white whooping crane in the flock.

And I have traveled along the contours
of leaves that have no name. Here
where the air is wet and the light is cool,

I feel what others are thinking and do not speak,
I know pleasure in the veins of a sugar maple,
I am living at the edge of a new leaf.

O

ORIGINAL MEMORY

1   White orchids along the window –
she notices something has nibbled the eggplant leaves,

mantises have not yet hatched from the egg.
"*Traduttori, traditori,*" said a multilinguist

discussing the intricacies of Hopi time and space,
but the inadvertent resonance in the mind

is that passion is original memory:
she is at the window pointing to Sagittarius,

she is slicing *porcini* and laying them in a pan,
she is repotting a cereus wearing chalcedony and gold earrings,

she is judging kachinas and selecting the simplest
to the consternation of museum employees.

Grilled shrimp in olive oil –
a red sensation pours into his thought and touch:

the sfumato of her face,
shining black hair reaching down to her waist,

he knows without looking the plum
bruises on her thigh from the spikes of a sectional warp.

2   The multilinguist wants to reveal the locations
of shrines on the salt trail in the Grand Canyon

but has been declared persona non grata by the tribe.
He may have disproved the thesis that the Hopi language

has no referents to time, but his obsession led
to angers and accusations, betrayals and pentimenti:

a cry of a nuthatch vanishes into aquamarine air.
Some things you have to see by making a pinhole,

holding a white sheet of paper at the proper focal length?
To try to retrace the arc of a passion is to

try to dream in slow motion a bursting into flame?
You are collecting budding yellow tea plants;

I am feeling a sexual splendor in a new orchid leaf.
What is the skin of the mind?

How do you distinguish "truth" from "true perception"?
When is an apex a nadir and a nadir an opening into a first world?

Italians slice *porcini*, lay them on screens in the sun,
let the maggots wriggle out and drop to the ground.

3   She is tipping water out of a cloud.
    By candlelight, face to face,

    the pleasures of existence are caught in a string of pearls.
    He remembers her rhythm in a corn dance,

    notices the swelling of her left ear from a new earring.
    He does not want any distortion –

    red leaves falling or beginning to fall,
    bright yellow chamisa budding along a dirt road,

    snow accumulating on black branches –
    to this moment of chiaroscuro in which their lives are a sphere.

    Face to face, by candlelight,
    the rock work and doorways form a series of triptychs.

    She remembers hiking the trail up to Peñasco Blanco,
    sees the Chuska Mountains violet in the west,

    and, below, the swerve of Chaco Wash,
    the canyon opening up: ruins of rock walls

    calcined in the heat, and, in red light,
    swallows gathering and daubing mud along the cliff face.

1   I walk along the length of a stone-and-gravel garden
       and feel without looking how the fifteen stones
       appear and disappear. I had not expected the space
       to be defined by a wall made of clay boiled in oil
       nor to see above a series of green cryptomeria
       pungent in spring. I stop and feel an April snow
       begin to fall on the stones and raked gravel and see
       how distance turns into abstraction desire and ordinary
       things: from the air, corn and soybean fields are
       a series of horizontal and vertical stripes of pure color:
       viridian, yellow ocher, raw sienna, sap green. I
       remember in Istanbul at the entrance to the Blue Mosque
       two parallel, extended lines of shoes humming at
       the threshold of paradise. Up close, it's hard to know
       if the rattle of milk bottles will become a topaz,
       or a moment of throttled anger, tripe that is
       chewed and chewed. In the distance, I feel drumming
       and chanting and see a line of Pueblo women dancing
       with black-on-black jars on their heads; they lift
       the jars high then start to throw them to the ground.

2 Rope at ankle level,
a walkway sprinkled with water
under red and orange maples along a white-plastered wall;

moss covering the irregular ground
under propped-up weeping cherry trees;

in a corral
a woman is about to whisper and pat the roan's neck;

an amber chasm inside a cello;

in a business conversation,
the silences are eel farms passed on a bullet train;

a silence in the shape of a rake;

a sheet of ice floating along a dock;
the texture of icy-black basil leaves at sunrise;

a shaggymane pushing up through asphalt;

a woman wearing a multicolored dress of silk-screened
  naked women
about to peel an egg;

three stones leading into a pond.

3 Desire is to memory as an azalea is to a stone?
During the Cultural Revolution, the youngest brother
of the Peng family was executed against a wall
in Chengdu for being a suspected Guomindang agent.
Years earlier, the eldest brother was executed
at that wall for being a suspected communist.
This Chengdu effect has no end, but if you interiorize,
a series of psychological tragedies
has the resonance of stone-and-gravel waterfalls.
A first frost sweetens the apples; I want them sweeter
but discover a second frost makes the cores mush;
so essential shapes are destroyed starting at the center.
A woman and man must ache from a series of betrayals
before they can begin to bicker at the dinner table.
I water hyacinth bulbs planted in shallow pots
in the cool, dark bathroom, and, though it feels
odd to do so when walnuts are rotting on the ground,
a thought of spring is inadvertent pleasure:
a policeman pushed a dancer against a car, said, "Sure,"
when he insisted he had marigolds, not marijuana.

4   She puts jars in a pit, covers them with sawdust,
adds a layer of shards and covers them,
builds a fire, and, when the burn is intense,
smothers it with sheep dung. She will not know
for a few hours if the jars have turned completely
black and did not break cooling. For now,
no one sees or knows; I inhale smoke, see
vendors along the docks selling grilled
corn smelling of charcoal, the air at dusk
plangent with cries from minarets up on the hill –
the cries resembling the waves of starlings
that always precede the pulsing wing-beat Vs
of sandhill cranes. Oh, you can glow with anger,
but it leaves the soot of an oil burner
on the windows and walls. If anguish is an end
in itself, you walk into a landscape of
burned salt cedar along a river. I remember
seeing hungry passengers disembark at the docks.

5   Men dressed in cottonwood leaves dance
     in the curving motion of a green rattlesnake.
     I am walking along a sandstone trail
     and stop in a field of shards: here is a teal zigzag
     and there is a blood-red deer's breath arrow.
     Women dancers offer melons to the six directions
     then throw them to the ground. A wave
     rocks through the crowd as the melons are smashed open.
     I know I have walked along a path lit
     by candles inside open-mesh cast-iron carp.
     I stop at a water basin, and as I bend to
     ladle water, see reflected, a sweet gum leaf.
     As a cornmeal path becomes a path to the gods
     then a cornmeal path again, I see the line
     of women dancing with black-on-black jars on their heads.
     They raise the jars with macaw and lightning patterns
     to the six directions then form a circle
     and throw them down on the center-marking stones.

6   "Go kiss a horse's ass."

"He hanged himself from the flagpole."

"I just do what I'm told."

She wanted him to hold her and say nothing.

"Depression is due to loss or guilt."

Who heard shrieks?
In the morning,
a mutilated body was found behind the adobe church.

He saw that "A or B" was not a choice since A and B had been
    predetermined.

"I hated that painting painting so I burned it."

Hair on the woodstove.

"I'm so glad."

After fallopian surgery, she touches her scar, combs her hair,
    puts on makeup.

The red phoenix tattoos on the arms of a locksmith.

"A man's character is his fate."

He had two cameras but was always pawning one to release
the other.

They slept a Mediterranean sleep: sun, sand, water;
the bed had the soft motion of waves.

"No, no, no, no, no, no, no!"

"Water is the koan of water."

7   I look at fourteen stones submerged at varying depths
     in a sea of gravel. I do not know under which stone
     is a signature but guess that a pin-sized hourglass space,
     separating intention and effect, is a blind point
     where anger may coalesce into a pearl. I may sit here
     until the stones have a riparian shine and are buoyant
     in September starlight, yet never live to see
     how grief turns into the effortless stretch of a fisherman
     casting a fly onto a stream. When I slept on the float house
     I became accustomed to the rise and fall of the tide,
     so that when I walked on the rain forest island
     I was queasy. I wanted a still pellucid point
     but realize the necessary and sufficient condition
     is to feel the pin-sized space as a point of resistance,
     as a smash that is a beginning wave of light.
     The dancers reappear and enter the plaza in two lines.
     Shifting feet in rhythm to the shifting drumming,
     they approach the crowd under the yellow cottonwood.